HEYDAYS, FAIR-DAYS
———— AND ————
NOT-SO-GOOD OLD DAYS

For my brother Stanley, another exile from Fermanagh

The Friar's Bush Press gratefully acknowledges the
support of the Fermanagh District Council in making
this publication possible.

The Friar's Bush Press
24 College Park Avenue,
Belfast 7
Published 1986
© Copyright reserved
ISBN   0   946872   05   8

Book design—Spring Graphics, Saintfield
Typesetting—Compuset, Belfast
Printing—Universities Press

W·A·MAGUIRE

◆ HEYDAYS ◆
FAIR-DAYS
AND NOT-SO-GOOD
OLD DAYS

*A Fermanagh estate and village in the
photographs of the Langham family, 1890—1918*

The History of
TEMPO MANOR

Tempo House c 1865

One

THE MAGUIRES

THE AREA AROUND the village of Tempo in County Ferman-agh was part of a large estate called the manor of Inseloghagease (named after Lough Eyes nearby) granted by King James I during the plantation of Ulster to Brian Maguire. Brian was a younger brother of Hugh (chief 1589-1600) and also of Cuchonnacht, who organised the 'flight of the earls'—which provided the English government with the opportunity to confiscate most of Ulster. Unlike Cuchonnacht, Brian was determined to make the best of the new situation, and was one of the first of the grantees to settle on his new estate. By August 1611 he had built a substantial house surrounded by a bawn or fortified enclosure. His younger brother Tirlagh got a smaller estate nearby, which passed to Brian on Tirlagh's death a few years later. In this way, Brian Maguire became the owner of a property which was pretty extensive, though much of it was either rough hill grazing or heavily wooded. In the barony of Tirkennedy, as that part of north-east Fermanagh was called when the former 'Maguire's Country' was made into an English county, the Maguire estate consisted of over forty modern townlands stretching from Tullyweel in the east to beyond Tempo in the west and northwards as far as the border with Tyrone—an area of 13-14,000 acres. In addition there were two separate pieces of property in south Fermanagh, in the barony of Clanawley, amounting to another 2,000 acres or so. Though named Inseloghagease in the grant, the manor did not include Lough Eyes and almost from the beginning it was referred to as Tempodessell or Tempo instead.

Unlike the other Maguires who got grants of land in the plantation, Brian managed to hold on to his property, even under Cromwell. When he died in his castle at Tullyweel in 1655 he was the last remaining Irish landowner in Fermanagh. He had achieved this remarkable feat by living prudently and supporting the government. He even sent warning to the governor of Enniskillen in 1641 that his kinsmen were helping to organise the rebellion that broke out in that year—and during the troubled time that followed he was lucky not to fall victim to the wrath of one side or the other. His only son Hugh took a different course and was killed fighting against the English in 1650.

The first house and bawn built by Brian Maguire in the early seventeenth century may have been at Tullyweel rather than Tempo. No sign now remains of that house, but the ruins were marked on nineteenth century maps. Sir William Petty's map, however, which was based on the survey he carried out under Cromwell during the 1650s, shows a castle at 'Templedisell' (Tempo), and there is also a reference by an eye-witness to Brian Maguire's house at 'Templedassett' in the 1640s. It seems that he built two houses or castles, at either end of his property, though it is certainly true that during the seventeenth century the Maguires of Tempo lived much of the time at Tullyweel.

Brian Maguire was succeeded in 1655 by his five-year-old grandson Cuchonnacht, who grew up to be an expensive young man living well beyond the modest income his estate provided at that time. He borrowed heavily from his protestant neighbours and sold most of the land in south Fermanagh. By the time he died in 1691, half of the property was in the hands of his creditors and his debts amounted to many times the income. Some of the money had been used to raise a regiment of infantry to fight for King James II, for Cuchonnacht was a devoted jacobite and had been appointed high sheriff of Fermanagh under James. At the battle of Aughrim in 1691 Cuchonnacht was killed with most of his men. According to family tradition, one of his followers cut off Cuchonnacht's head, put it in a sack and brought it back to Fermanagh, where he buried it on the island of Devenish in Lough Erne.

Because he had died in arms against the new king, William III, Cuchonnacht was declared a traitor after his death and his

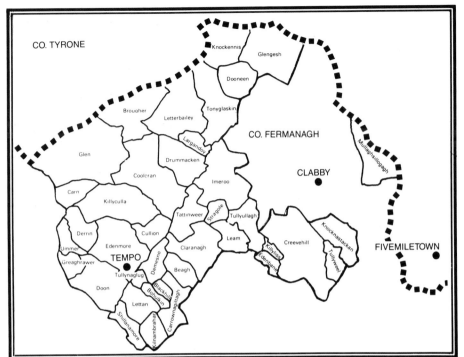

Tempo Manor estate in the barony of Tirkennedy, Co. Fermanagh in the early eighteenth century (names and divisions are modern townlands).
Drawn by D. Crone.
© *W.A. Maguire*

Having been restored to his property, which remained very heavily encumbered by his father's debts, Brian Maguire proceeded to marry Bridget Nugent, the wealthy daughter of Colonel James Nugent of Coolamber, County Longford, and to use her dowry to pay off most of the creditors. He died at Tullyweel in 1712, when only in his mid-thirties, lamented not only by his family but also by the gaelic scribes and harpers whom he had patronised. The famous blind harper Carolan is known to have visited Brian at Tempo (or Tullyweel) in 1708. Carolan's association with the family continued for the rest of his life, particularly when Brian's eldest son Cuchonnacht (usually referred to in English sources as Constantine) grew up and became the head of the family. One of Carolan's surviving airs, *Plangstai Milic Uidhir* (Planxty Maguire) was written for young Constantine.

Constantine had a reputation for hospitality. By the time he died unmarried in 1739 he had sold an outlying part of the Tempo estate and had borrowed substantial sums on the security of the rest. He was succeeded by his brother Robert. Under the penal laws passed by the protestant Irish parliament in the early eighteenth century, a Roman Catholic landowner was forbidden to bequeath his land by will: when he died, it was to be divided equally among all his sons. If the eldest conformed to the established church, however, he got the whole estate. Faced with the choice between conforming to the Church of Ireland and having their property broken up into smaller and

estates were confiscated. In 1694 they were granted to James Corry of Castlecoole, an ancestor of the earls of Belmore. William's English parliament, however, disapproved of the way he had disposed of so much confiscated Irish land to his Dutch favourites and eventually, in 1700, forced him to cancel all the grants and to set up a board of trustees to hear petitions from claimants and to sell any property that remained. The late owner of Tempo had married Mary Magennis of Castlewellan in 1675 and had four sons, the eldest of whom, Brian, now claimed the estates on the grounds that his father had had only a life interest. He succeeded in proving this claim before the trustees, who restored the family property to him in 1702, making it one of the very few Ulster estates to have survived all the upheavals of the seventeenth century, and to have remained in the hands of the original gaelic owners.

smaller pieces, many Roman Catholic families preferred to conform. The Maguires of Tempo were no exception. Robert conformed in 1739, his brother Hugh a few years later. In 1741 Robert married Elizabeth McDermott Roe, only child and heiress of Henry McDermott Roe of Greyfield, County Roscommon. Her large dowry, 4,000 guineas, should have helped to clear the Tempo estate of debt. Most of it was probably not paid, however, and then the Greyfield estate itself was lost by the extravagance of Elizabeth's father (who ended up by living with his daughter at Tempo, where he died in 1752).

The person who acquired Greyfield, by foreclosing his mortgage on it, was Robert Maguire's younger brother Hugh. If even half the accounts of Hugh Maguire are true, he was a desperado to outdesperado anything in fiction. After serving in the Austrian army as a young man he returned to England in the early 1740s. In 1745 he married, as her fourth husband, the wealthy Lady Cathcart, who purchased a colonel's

commission for him and endowed him with half the income from her property. Her money was used—on her own behalf, through trustees—to buy up all the mortgages and other securities affecting a large part of the Tempo estate from Constantine's time, at a cost of more than £8,000. In 1751, on behalf of himself and his wife, Hugh sued his brother Robert, the nominal owner, for these debts, and in 1755 the court ordered that the money should be repaid or the property sold. It is very difficult to disentangle what actually happened, but there is no doubt that until his death in 1766 Hugh was the effective owner of most of the Fermanagh estate. Even as early as 1749 he seems to have been in control, for the Royal Society in Dublin awarded a prize in that year to Colonel Hugh Maguire for planting trees at Tempo. It appears that by his will (1766) Hugh left Tempo to his brothers Robert and Philip.

Not only did Hugh Maguire acquire and dispose of the McDermott Roe estate in Roscommon and become the squire

The old house at Tempo in 1853

'The old house at Tempo in 1853', from a watercolour sketch (Public Record Office of Northern Ireland). This curious building dated from the time of Hugh Maguire who sold it in 1799. None of the new owners of the estate lived in the house, but it was inhabited by stewards and agents for some years, and by William Tennent's brother Robert and his family occasionally for holidays.

of Tempo, but he also acquired property in Longford and Westmeath. In fact he seems to have lived for most of his later years at Castle Nugent in County Longford, an estate which perhaps came to him through his mother Bridget Nugent. The *Dublin Journal*, reporting her death there at the age of seventy-seven in December 1754, described Castle Nugent as 'the seat of Col. Maguire'. We also know that Hugh Maguire was a member of the grand jury for Westmeath from 1750 to 1763 and served as high sheriff of the county in 1754. To put the matter beyond any doubt, legal documents relating to his widow the former Lady Cathcart refer to her as 'the relict of Hugh Maguire formerly of Castlenugent in the Co. of Longford Esq. deceased'.

The wicked colonel was notorious in his own day and became a fictional villain for all time because of his treatment of his wife. Far from being satisfied with half of her considerable income, he did his worst to frighten her into handing over a fortune in jewels and the title deeds of her English property, the manor of Tewin Water in Hertfordshire. When she refused, he abducted her to Ireland and kept her locked up for years. Though there must have been a good deal of talk among the neighbours, no one dared to interfere; duelling was common and Maguire was a noted shot. After his death Lady Cathcart, then well over seventy, was released, ragged, half-starved and almost deranged. She recovered to live to the age of ninety-seven. Lady Cathcart's own story of how her husband died was like the climax to a gothic novel. Having eventually forced her to tell him that the deeds were in a secret compartment behind the panelling at Tewin, Maguire hurried there, entered the room and stood on a table to reach the hidden door. The rusty lock resisted all his efforts so, impatient to get what he wanted, he took a jack knife and forced the panel. The knife slipped and cut his hand badly. Lockjaw followed and he died in agony shortly afterwards.

The imprisonment of Lady Cathcart is supposed to have happened at Tempo. The room where she was kept, in what later became an outbuilding, was pointed out to visitors in the nineteenth century and can still be seen. The great Irish writer Maria Edgeworth based the character of Sir Kit Rackrent in her novel *Castle Rackrent* on Hugh Maguire, for the story of Lady Cathcart and her adventures was made known in her obituary in the *Gentleman's Magazine* in 1789. Furthermore, when he lived at Castle Nugent the colonel was a near neighbour of the Edgeworths.

After Hugh Maguire's death his brother Robert re-emerged as head of the family. It was he who sold the last of the property in south Fermanagh (Beagh and Monyauragan) to the Coles of Florencecourt in 1770, and there is a lease from him to a tenant at Tempo dated 1773. He and his wife Elizabeth had no children. The next male relations were his surviving brother Philip and Philip's son Hugh (born *c* 1750). In 1777, the year before he died, Robert joined with Philip in settling the Tempo estate on Hugh in return for an annuity for himself and a sum of £4,000 for Philip.

Little is known about Philip Maguire. So far as one can gather, he lived for most of his life in Dublin and died there in 1789. His wife Frances Morres came from a well-connected family in Tipperary, her mother being a daughter of Richard Talbot of Malahide and her sister Helen becoming countess of Ormond and Ossory. As well as their only son Hugh they had two daughters, the elder of whom married Owen O'Reilly of Mount Pallas in County Cavan; the other became the wife of John Stuart Hamilton of Donemana, County Tyrone, who was made an Irish baronet in 1780.

From 1777 to 1800 the head of the family and the owner of Tempo was Hugh Maguire. In 1773 he married Phoebe Macnamara from Cong, County Mayo, whose family was connected with the Butlers, the Talbots and other notable families. They had three sons—Constantine, Brian and Stephen—and five daughters. When one of the daughters, Maria, married a nobleman from Padua and became the marchesa of Zigno Patavino, she had little difficulty in producing the sixteen heraldic quarterings needed to gain her entry to the imperial court at Vienna. Hugh Maguire seems to have inherited his wicked uncle's property in Longford and Westmeath, and possibly lived for a time at Castle Nugent before selling it. He settled at Tempo and was a popular figure in Fermanagh society, serving as high sheriff of the county in 1780. By all accounts the name bestowed on an earlier Maguire,

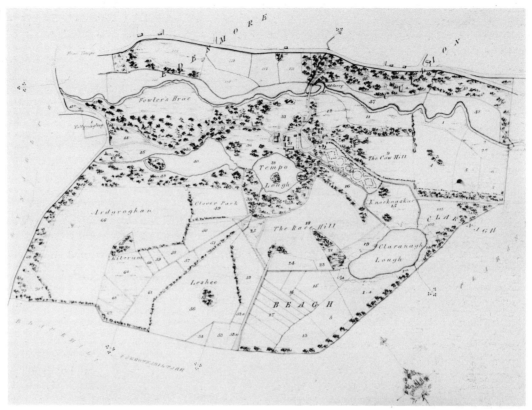

Demesne of Tempo, drawn by Robert Montgomery in 1844.

Hugh the Hospitable, could equally have been his, for he entertained lavishly. The Irish scholar John O'Donovan, who visited Tempo in the 1830s when working for the ordnance survey, described him as 'one of the most puissant, high-minded and accomplished gentlemen that ever came of the Maguire family'.

O'Donovan went on to say, however, that Hugh mortgaged Tempo and left his family in great distress. The fact is, he lived far beyond his means. Though the property he got from his uncle Robert in 1777 still included most of the estate granted to Brian Maguire in 1610, it was heavily encumbered by debt. In particular, the debts created in the 1720s and 1730s by Constantine, which Lady Cathcart's trustees had taken over in the 1740s, had never been paid and now amounted to the sum of nearly £11,000. In order to put a stop to 'all further controversies and litigation concerning the same', Hugh in 1778 admitted liability for the sum of £10,804 and gave Lady Cathcart a mortgage secured on some thirty townlands of the estate. After her death in 1789, her trustees sued for payment and eventually, in 1799, forced the sale of just over 2,000 Irish (3,277 statute) acres. This was more than two-thirds of what then remained, and included the house and demesne of Tempo and most of the village. The purchaser was a linen merchant from Derry named Samuel Lyle, who paid £20,000.

Hugh had succeeded in postponing that nemesis for most of his life (he died a year later, in October 1800) but only by creating further debts on his own account and by selling other substantial portions of the estate. Seven townlands were mortgaged in 1783; five years later John Richards of Dublin bought ten whole townlands and parts of another three for some £12,000; two others were sold in 1798. By 1800, all that remained to the Maguires were 818 Irish (1,325 statute) acres, which at that time produced a rent of about £350 a year. Towards the end of his life Hugh Maguire also went off the rails morally: according to O'Donovan he turned out his wife Phoebe and lived with a housemaid.

Constantine Maguire, Hugh's eldest son, inherited this sadly diminished estate. His mother soon had to take him to court for failing to pay her dower, which was secured on the property. Thereafter they were not on speaking terms. In 1817, she inherited the property of an uncle and took the name Butler in addition to Maguire; she died in Dublin in 1829. Constantine, known locally around Tempo as Captain Cohonny, may actually have held a commission in the army (his daughter was born in the garrison town of Athlone in 1805) but no details of his early life are known except for a story that when he and his younger brother Brian were boys they used to put apples on each other's heads and shoot them off with pistols. Constantine turned up at Tempo from time to time after the family home had been sold; as lord of the manor still, with certain rights over the whole property, he must have been rather a nuisance to the new owners. For several years before and after 1820 he negotiated with William Tennent (Lyle's successor) either to buy back or to lease the house and demesne, but all his schemes fell through for lack of money. Relations between the two men became so strained that in August 1828 they were only prevented from fighting a duel when the authorities got to hear of it and bound them over to keep the peace. In 1829, following a dispute with some of his Tempo tenants, Constantine was fired at by a local Orangeman named Rutledge, who had the bad luck to be shipwrecked after setting out for America to escape trial for

attempted murder. When the survivors were rescued and brought ashore at Cork, Rutledge was arrested on the quayside by Constantine and the law, taken under guard to Enniskillen and subsequently hanged there. After that, Constantine came no more to Tempo but instead went to live in Tipperary, on a small property he had inherited. There, one morning after breakfast in 1834, he was found murdered on his front lawn. His assassins, more successful than their counterparts in Fermanagh, were never detected. Married in 1804 to a Scotswoman, Frances Augusta Maclean, he had one daughter, Florence Elizabeth, who later married an anglican clergyman named Brereton. There was also a son Hugh, born about 1820 whose legitimacy was never accepted by his uncle Brian, according to O'Donovan. Nevertheless, after being educated at Portora Royal School and King's Inns, Dublin (where he was entered as a student in 1840), he appears to have inherited what was left of the family property, for the government valuation of 1862 shows Hugh Maguire as the owner of some 900 acres in the Tempo area.

Constantine's brother Brian derived considerable benefit from the target practice the two of them had as boys. He grew up to be a notorious duellist and wild man, whom even the army of the East India Company could not tolerate. His memoirs, published in Dublin in 1811, were rapidly withdrawn from circulation by his more respectable friends. They read like fiction and to a large extent probably were. He was a famous, and rather dangerous, 'character' in Dublin for many years, before declining into destitution and ill-health in the 1830s. He ended his days in 1835 in a shed at Finglas, with no possessions but his sword and pistols, and no company except his younger son and the mummified remains of the elder one. The latter gruesome companion he was said to have preserved by some secret means learned on his travels. The surviving son, Charles, went to sea as a common sailor and disappeared. According to one account, it was his two grandsons who turned up at Tempo in the early years of the present century, having come from Australia to claim what was left of the family property. Both died in the county asylum without heirs. According to another version, these unfortunates were descendants of Constantine's son Hugh. Either way they were ghosts from the past, whose appearance in Tempo called to mind old tales of a curse on the family and O'Donovan's remark that its downfall was caused by war, women and madness.

Seal of Constantine Maguire (c 1775-1834). Drawn by D. Crone.

Two
THE TENNENTS
and
THE LANGHAMS

SAMUEL LYLE, the linen merchant from Derry who had purchased most of Hugh Maguire's remaining estate in 1799, sold the property fifteen years later. He never lived at Tempo, but visited his estate regularly in order to collect the rents himself; on these occasions he stayed at the village inn, where he kept a furnished room. Although he did not reside at Tempo, Lyle apparently grew fond of the place. In a letter to William Tennent, the next owner, in July 1813, he wrote: 'Now that I am speaking of the Demesne, it is one of the most beautiful spots you ever saw, wood and water most delightfully disposed and in the very heart of the estate; if it had been possible for me to leave the County of Derry I would have gone there to live. You may have a dish of fish out of the river or leeks every day of the year, plenty of crawfish in the river, also plenty of game, in short I think the Demesne would give a family everything but wine and groceries . . .'.

Like Lyle, the new owner was a merchant from the other

William Tennent (1759-1832), the Belfast banker who bought the Tempo estate in 1814, by an unknown artist.

(Ulster Museum, Belfast)

end of the province. William Tennent was the son of a presbyterian minister from Roseyards near Ballymoney, County Antrim. He made a fortune in sugar refining and various trading activities in Belfast before establishing, in 1809, the Commercial Bank (subsequently amalgamated with the Belfast Banking Company, itself now part of the Northern Bank). Like many Ulster presbyterians of the time, he held radical political views; arrested in 1798 as a suspected leader of the United Irishmen, he was imprisoned at Fort George in Scotland for almost four years. This did not prevent him from becoming one of the leading citizens of Belfast in later years, prominent in education and public welfare as well as in the Chamber of Commerce. Neither did his being a prominent member of the First Presbyterian congregation in Rosemary Street prevent him from having, in addition to two legitimate daughters, a large illegitimate family, all of whom he acknowledged and provided for. Some of his wealth was invested in landed property, not only the Tempo estate—for which he paid Lyle the large sum of £29,000 (well over a million in modern money)—but also land in Tyrone, Donegal and Sligo. He might well have sold Tempo again, either to Constantine Maguire or someone else, if the value of the land had not fallen so badly in the 1820s. His attitude to being a landowner was expressed to one enquirer in 1832 as follows: 'Having been bred a merchant, I am not at all displeased at being asked to sell any property I have, whether lands or merchandise . . .'.

During Lyle's time, the demesne at Tempo was let. Hugh Maguire's house, uninhabited during these years, decayed rapidly. This curious building consisted of two wings different in appearance and probably built at different dates, connected by a single-storey section. It was assessed by the hearth money collector in 1818 as having ten hearths and thirty-two windows. Tennent decided to repair it in 1816, and used it for occasional short visits when in Fermanagh on business or when attending the assizes as a grand juror of the county. He also repaired the manor pew in the parish church, and provided new gates for the churchyard. The repaired Tempo House, however, was mostly used for summer holidays by Tennent's brother Dr Robert Tennent and his family, who came regularly from 1817

onward. Dr Tennent's daughter Jane kept accounts of expenditure on these visits, some of which have survived. Jane's accounts for their first visit in 1817 give interesting glimpses of the cost of travel from Belfast (a total of £3. 12s. 11d., of which £1. 3s. 9d. was spent on fodder for the horses and 3s. 4d. on a pint of port); of the cost of household items bought locally (3 shillings for six egg cups, 13 shillings for a gallon of whiskey, 6s. 8d. for eight loaves); and of poverty among the people ('a poor woman with bilberries 10d.', or 'gave a little Boy for trout 5d.').

The agent's letters during these years also tell of desperate poverty, or worse. 'Famine seems to approach if God do not avert it', he wrote in November 1816. Tennent's agent for the first ten years was the Church of Ireland curate Henry Leard, who lived at Pubble. Leard seems to have spent much of his time in farming—he leased the demesne from Tennent and dealt in cattle—when not pursuing the tenants for rent. He was not slow to ask his employer for favours. When the post office was established at Tempo in 1821, he got Tennent to nominate his brother as postmaster; and, when he heard that Tennent was likely to become high sheriff of Fermanagh, he proposed himself as sub-sheriff. His letters, many of which survive with Tennent's replies scribbled on them, are a mine of interesting information about the estate during these difficult postwar years, when Tennent seriously considered selling it because it yielded so little income.

When Tennent died of cholera during an outbreak of the disease in Belfast in 1832, his daughters Letitia and Isabella inherited his property. A dispute about the terms of the will led to a prolonged lawsuit which ended in 1839 when James Emerson Tennent, Letitia's husband, was obliged to purchase her life interest in order to secure control of it. As M.P. for Belfast (later Lisburn) and holder of various political offices, his career lay elsewhere—even for five years, in Ceylon, where he was civil secretary to the governor from 1845 to 1850—so there was no question of his living at Tempo. He was greatly attached to the place, however, and took a close interest in seeing that the estate was well run by a reliable agent named Thomas Adams. In his later years Adams lived in part of the house, as well as leasing the demesne. Some of his letters also survive. He

gave his employer good advice, for example in 1835 warning him against raising money by letting strangers purchase leases over the heads of the tenants who actually farmed the land. He could be very blunt, and deserved to sign himself 'Plain Thos. Adams'. This, and the strength of his evangelical protestant beliefs, comes through clearly in the following letter in 1838:

'I have lived a good part of my life without writing letters on the sabbath day till I got acquainted with gentlemen, and parliament men, but guessing the anxiety of your spirit I bend to satisfy you. Pray for my forgiveness, and for your own prosperity in spiritual as well as temporal things. It is right to be diligent in business, fervent in spirit serving the Lord, but all this will not excuse me of sabbathbreaking'.

In his later years Sir James Emerson Tennent, as he had become, took an increasingly close interest in Tempo—unlike his son William, to whom the estate was to pass. As his father wrote to him in 1861: 'You dislike a country life, and I enjoy one. You dislike the management of the Tempo Estate, and I have great pleasure in it. You have an aversion to the idea of passing any time there, whilst it is one of the objects of my life and one of your mother's dearest wishes to have a Cottage there . . .'.

So it was that the present house came to be built, to designs by the eminent Belfast architect, Sir Charles Lanyon. The main part of the building was completed in 1864, the billiard room and tower being added three years later, when Sir James retired from his post as secretary to the Board of Trade and at last went

James Emerson Tennent (1804-69), from a contemporary engraving (Ulster Museum, Belfast). The third son of a Belfast merchant named Emerson, he married William Tennent's daughter Letitia in 1831 and took the name Tennent as an additional surname. During the Greek war of independence in the 1820s, he visited Greece and met Lord Byron. Elected M.P. for Belfast for most of the period 1832-45, and later for Lisburn, he was knighted in 1845 and made a baronet in 1867. He was also a successful writer (his two-volume book on Ceylon sold five editions in less than a year) and a Fellow of the Royal Society.

to live in his 'cottage'. In fact, despite being rather larger than most cottages, the house Lanyon designed really did have something of the character of one, with its curly gables and its high Tudor-style twisted chimneys (now gone but visible in old photographs). Before his death in 1869 Sir James also laid out most of the gardens around the house, though much was added later by the Langhams.

Sir William Emerson Tennent married in 1870 and died only six years later at the age of forty-one, leaving a widow and two small daughters. The widow later married Cavendish Butler, who lived on Inishrath in Upper Lough Erne. The elder of the two daughters, Ethel (known to her family and friends as Jenny), eventually inherited the Tempo estate. In 1893 she married Charles Langham, heir to a baronetcy and an estate at Cottesbrooke in Northamptonshire. Charles Langham came to live at Tempo, and liked it so well that after he succeeded his father in 1909 he sold Cottesbrooke (a fine property but heavily encumbered by his father's extravagant passion for hunting) and stayed on for the rest of his life. His early affection for the place is obvious enough in his photographs of the house and demesne. What is equally obvious from his pictures of local people, is that as a newcomer he was shocked by the poverty and destitution of many of them. Sir Charles and Lady Langham died within a few weeks of each other in 1951. The present (fifteenth) baronet, Sir James, is their grandson.

Many of the interests of Charles and Jenny Langham are reflected in the photographs printed here—natural history, gardening, travel and motor cars, as well as photography itself. Though by no means enormously rich, they lived very comfortably and could afford to indulge their tastes. In the late 1890s and early 1900s Charles Langham was mainly interested in photography. Later, natural history was his absorbing passion. He became one of the great amateur collectors, particularly of butterflies. During the 1920s and 1930s the Langhams roamed Europe in search of new specimens. There were more butterflies in Europe (and Ireland) than there are now. On a trip to the Alps in 1926 the Langhams could be sure of finding specimens of Nogel's Hairstreak, the Sooty Copper, the Alcon Blue, Iolas Blue, Damon Blue, the Green Underside Blue, the Blackeyed Blue, Amanda's Blue, the Spanish Chalkhill Blue and the Geranium Argus—all now endangered or extinct. The first signs of the collecting urge can be seen in the photograph of Jenny Langham with butterfly nets in the south of France. Another interest of her husband's, more common among country gentlemen of his day (who spent much of their time shooting them), was birds. Tempo House as shown here had an aviary of live birds, as well as a fine collection of stuffed ones—not to mention a range of wild birds' eggs that would have been any schoolboy's dream. Fortunately, the results of his life's work as a naturalist, in the original mounts and cases that he provided, have been preserved and are now in the Ulster Museum, Belfast. His other memorial, no less interesting, is the photographs.

View of the new house c 1865, from the driveway which at that time led from the house to the Clabby road, crossing the Tempo river and the millrace by the rustic bridges shown here.

Three
The Village of
TEMPO

ACCORDING TO to King James's attorney general in Ireland, Sir John Davies, at the time of the Ulster plantation there was not a single fixed town or village in the whole of Fermanagh. This was because the Irish inhabitants were cattle farmers rather than cultivators, and moved about with their herds. The introduction of the English system of landholding, and the spread of tillage farming, gradually changed this state of affairs and led to the development of small settlements as centres of estates and local markets.

So far as we know, the village of Tempo scarcely existed at all in the seventeenth century but grew up later in the townland of Edenmore, close to the fortified house built by Brian Maguire and beside his manor mill on the twisting Tempo river. (The name Tempo, *An tIompu Deiseal* in Irish, means a turn to the right and may derive from this natural feature—or possibly from an ancient association with sun worship ritual). Indeed, until the latter part of the eighteenth century the village, such as it was, was called Milltown. As well as the manor mill in Edenmore townland, at which all the tenants of the estate were obliged to grind their corn, the marriage settlement of Robert Maguire and Elizabeth McDermott Roe in 1741 mentions tuck mills (for fulling woollen cloth) in Cullion and Ardgroghan nearby.

The only church in the area was a small thatched chapel some distance away at Pubble, site of a pre-Reformation church and graveyard, which was used by protestant worshippers until the vestry of the parish of Enniskillen (of which the area was

Parish church and houses at the west end of Tempo c 1865. This is the earliest picture of the village.

then a part) decided to build the present church at Tempo in the 1780s. Hugh Maguire, himself a member of the established church, gave the land. Roman Catholic worship survived easily enough under the protection of the Maguires, however, though reduced to using mass altars and temporary chapels. The Roman Catholic church in the village was built in 1826, the Methodist meeting house ten years later and the Presbyterian meeting house in the 1840s. A post office was opened in 1821 and a police barracks soon afterwards. A dispensary was also established about this time: there are several references in the letters of William Tennent's agent Leard to the doctors who served in Tempo. Tennent and Constantine Maguire also corresponded about setting up a school; certainly one had been established by the early 1830s.

The growth of the village in the late eighteenth century came with increasing population and the revival of the cattle trade. The Napoleonic wars increased the demand for grain as well. By the 1830s Tempo had become an important local market for grain, cattle and butter. James Emerson Tennent's agent Thomas Adams in 1835 was buying up considerable quantities of butter for shipment to England. He reported buying 85 firkins at Tempo market on 26 August, and wrote a month later that he had 'about 250 firkins to prepare and to send off for England'. The original grant of the manor to Brian Maguire had included the right to hold weekly markets and a Lammas fair. By the nineteenth century, the market at the end of each month had come to be known as the Fair. Those held in the spring and autumn were particularly important, since rents were due twice a year, in May and November, and landlords expected their tenants to pay out of the proceeds of the sales. The fair held on 28 May 1900 and photographed by the Langhams with their Kodak cameras was typical.

By 1834, when it was described as 'a collection of irregular houses, inhabited by farmers and labourers', Tempo had a population of 333 (170 Protestants and 163 Roman Catholics). In addition to its two churches, its police barracks and post office it had a chemist, two grocers, two bakers, three shoemakers, three carpenters, two coopers, two blacksmiths and twelve public houses. By 1841 there were 92 houses and 422

people. The number of inhabitants declined very slightly over the next decade, the years of the great potato famine. Thereafter it went on growing, to a peak of over 500 in the early 1860s, when there were 107 houses.

By the end of the century, however, when the Langhams were busy with their cameras, the village had declined drastically in size. All new building had long since ceased, the number of dwelling houses had fallen to 82 (and seven of those were uninhabited) and the population had shrunk almost by half to 284. The compilers of the 1901 census attributed the decline to 'emigration and removal'. It is clear from their figures that many men especially had been forced to seek work elsewhere, for the population that remained was composed of 166 females but only 118 males. Despite some roofless ruins, which illustrate the decline in population more vividly than any statistics, most of the houses in the Langhams' photographs appear nevertheless to be substantial and well-built, and the Fair Day pictures show a crowded and bustling scene. The fact is that while many people had left the village during the previous three decades, the modest prosperity of the remainder had been maintained by the improved position of local farmers (not farm labourers), to whom Gladstone's land laws gave lower rents and greater security. Shortly after these photographs were taken the appearance of the village was improved further, when the main street was tarmacadamed for the first time and electric street lighting was introduced.

The new house built by Sir James Emerson Tennent in 1863, photographed c 1865. The tower and billiard room were not added till 1867.

THE PHOTOGRAPHS

BEFORE THE 1880s photography was quite difficult for amateurs. The introduction of the dry plate process made the technique much simpler. More important, in 1888 George Eastman produced his Kodak box camera, with its spool of celluloid film which could be sent to the factory for processing. During the 1890s various other types of hand cameras appeared which made it possible to take pictures that were more candid and informal than those taken with larger cameras on tripods, for which sitters had to pose carefully.

All the photographs in this book come from the Langham family albums. Apart from the earliest, which date from the 1860s, most of them were taken by Charles Langham. Many of his portraits of local people have been copied from rather faded photographs for which no negatives survive, but the majority have been printed directly from the original negatives. Charles Langham—as one of the pictures here shows—sometimes used a plate camera with tripod, but most of the photographs were taken with a Kodak camera of the type used by thousands of amateurs. He and his wife were rather more successful with their snapshots than many amateurs, however. They not only took a lot of care in photographing their subjects but they also preserved the results carefully, mounting the larger prints in a professional manner and storing the smaller ones in Kodak albums, in which the square celluloid negatives were inserted underneath the prints themselves, where they remained quite safely for the next eighty years. Better still, the Langhams

Charles Langham c 1900 with his full-plate camera and tripod. Most of his portraits of the local people were taken with this camera or a similar one.

believed in documenting their work, so they identified the place, date and subject in nearly every case.

Up to a point, old photographs speak for themselves. How much they tell us, however, depends upon how well informed we are. Without some idea of who took them and when, and of who or what the subjects are, it is often difficult to know what to make of them. Provided we have these details, on the other hand, photographs better enable us to imagine the lives of people in the past than almost any other kind of historical evidence. Certainly these pictures speak volumes about life in Fermanagh eighty years ago, when the manor house was in its heyday, when the monthly fair was a great occasion in the village—and when too many local people had less than a decent living. The past really is a foreign country, the true strangeness of which is hidden from us by superficial similarities and lack of imagination. Through the recording eye of Charles Langham's camera we see the good and not-so-good old days of Tempo at the turn of the last century a little more clearly.

The value of this visual evidence is emphasised in the case of Tempo by the almost complete absence of it for any earlier period in the manor's history. There are no known portraits of any of the Maguires, only the seal of the unfortunate Constantine and the picture of the old house. At least we know what William Tennent and his son-in-law looked like, little though that knowledge may help us to imagine what it was like to live on their estate. For the two centuries before William Tennent became owner of part of it, the history of the manor can be told, however inadequately, only in words.

TEMPO HOUSE AND DEMESNE

THE ORIGINAL HOUSE on the site was the 'great copelled house' built about 1611 by Brian Maguire, to whom James I granted the manor of Inseloghagease during the plantation of Ulster. No trace of the original Tempo House can be identified, but the stables of the present one were part of an eighteenth century dwelling. The later Maguire house, reported in 1815 to be in a ruinous state, was repaired on several occasions but was beyond repair by 1861, when Sir James Emerson Tennent decided to replace it by a 'cottage'. Only some basement rooms and two nicely decorated chimneypieces from the Maguire house were incorporated in the rather grand cottage Sir Charles Lanyon designed for his client.

The demesne consisted of a little over a hundred acres, nearly forty of which were heavily wooded in 1814. The lovely gardens one sees today were also first laid out by Sir James Emerson Tennent. By the turn of the century, as these photographs show, they were already very attractive.

View of the house from the
west, May 1908, with Ethel
(Jenny) Langham and dogs.

Tempo House 23

Front and entrance, May
1908.

View of the back from
across the lake, May 1908.

Herbaceous border, June 1909

Backyard with thatched well, May 1908. The range of buildings across the yard was part of an earlier house. Above the door in the corner was the room where the wicked Colonel Hugh Maguire is said to have kept his wife (Lady Cathcart) confined for twenty years because she would not hand over her fortune.

Two views of the Brown Parlour in Tempo House, taken on 28 April 1912. The cabinet with shallow drawers on the left of the archway contained part of the butterfly collection, though most of the collection now in the Ulster Museum was built up later, in the 1920s. The portraits and armorial shields relate mostly to the history of the Langhams, whose baronetcy dates from 1660.

The Drawing Room, 28
April 1912, with its crystal
chandelier reflected in the
mantel mirror. The
transparent firescreens were
to shield the complexions of
the ladies from the direct
heat of the fire, without
obscuring its cheerful light.

The Dining Room, May 1908, with a fine collection of cut glass on the sideboard and a large wine cooler below.

'Jenny in the Rock Garden', 1901.

Charles Langham in his den, October 1899. The room contains signs of his own interest in natural history, and of his father's passion for foxhunting in Northamptonshire. The oriental figures on the mantel were brought from Ceylon by Sir James Emerson Tennent, Ethel Langham's grandfather, who was secretary to the governor of the island 1845-1850.

The Little Garden, July
1900.

The aviary at Tempo House, April 1904. The Langhams had a considerable collection of birds, including exotic pheasants and waterfowl as well as the fish eagle seen here.

'McKeagney mending the boat', April 1900. McKeagneys ran the forge in the village for many years, and the McKeagney family still lives and works in Tempo.

Sunday morning in the garden, July 1900. Ethel Langham (Jenny) is on the left, her mother Mrs Cavendish Butler on the right, with her sister-in-law Cecily Langham between.

Jenny (right) and Cecily Langham playing croquet at Tempo, June 1900.

Jenny Langham (right) with Cecily Langham and a visitor, June 1898.

Tempo House

Charles and Jenny Langham outside their front door in a 5 h.p. Garrard Tri-car, 19 March 1905. This two-cylinder machine had appeared on the market less than six months earlier, at a price of 125 guineas. A favourable review in the *Motor* of 25 October 1904 described the front seat as 'very comfortable and astonishingly free from vibration' and congratulated the designer of 'one of the best tri-car seats we have yet come across'. *The Motor Cycle* remarked that this type of vehicle was 'especially suitable for motor cyclists who sigh for companionship'.

The first aeroplane to land in County Fermanagh: a De Haviland VI biplane flying over Tempo House in 1918. The plane, from a Royal Air Force squadron stationed at Omagh, landed in the Big Field in the demesne on 13 October 1918. The pilot on that occasion was an American officer, B. W. Fryer from Manhattan. Three weeks later Capt. T. Weedon also landed. The Langhams had become friendly with some of the officers of the squadron, who established an air mail service using weighted pouches to drop messages. Some of the pouches and letters are still preserved in the house, along with a certificate recording the landings in the demesne.

This curious photograph was taken with a wide-angle landscape camera turned on end.

TEMPO VILLAGE

KNOWN UNTIL the middle of the eighteenth century or later as Milltown, because of its corn mill and tuck mills (for fulling woollen cloth), the village of Tempo began to grow thereafter as the cattle trade developed. The Church of Ireland parish church was built in the 1780s, the Roman Catholic church in 1826, Methodist and Presbyterian meeting houses a few years later. A post office was opened in 1821. Shortly afterwards a police barracks was established partly because of sectarian trouble in the area. By 1834, when it was described as 'a collection of irregular houses, inhabited by farmers and labourers', Tempo had a population of 333 and twelve pubs. The population reached a peak of over 500 thirty years later, but by the turn of the century it had shrunk to little more than half that figure. The original grant of the property included the right to hold weekly markets and a fair in August. By the nineteenth century, the last market in each month had come to be called the Fair. The one held on 28 May 1900, and photographed by the Langhams with their Kodak cameras, was particularly important because landlords expected tenants to pay their half-yearly rents out of the proceeds of the sales.

The main street looking west, 1 November 1899. The police barracks was in one of the houses on the right.

The view in the opposite direction, taken on the same day. The horse appears to be headless because its head has moved too fast for the speed of the camera shutter.

Tempo Village 43

Muldoon's Whiskey Shop
(one of 15) with Natives',
1899.

May Fair, 28 May 1900: a blind organgrinder with peg leg at the east end of the village.

May Fair: boys looking at the organgrinder. Lads like these were called 'caddies' locally; girls were known as 'cutties'.

May Fair: cattle sale, with
the Presbyterian meeting
house behind.

May Fair: a view down the
crowded main street.

May Fair: a scene at the Diamond.

May Fair: clothes sellers in the street. Most people in country areas at this date would have had their clothes made locally.

Orange procession in the
main street, 12 July 1900.

Waiting for the procession,
12 July 1900. The ruined
houses at this end of the
village illustrate the decline
in its population during the
previous thirty years.

Uniform variety: sergeant
and constables of the Royal
Irish Constabulary outside
their barracks in 1899.

LOCAL PEOPLE

THE LANGHAM photographs illustrate vividly the enormous difference between the lives of the family in the big house and the lives of ordinary people in rural Fermanagh at this time. Charles Langham himself was obviously struck by the poverty and wretchedness of some of the 'natives', as he called them. Indeed, his surviving pictures present an incomplete survey of the local population in this respect, for few of the more prosperous farmers—the sort who lived in two-storey thatched farmhouses rather than small cottages—appear in them. All the same, it is not hard to see why so many people emigrated from this part of Fermanagh, either to find work in Belfast or to the other side of the world. By 1900, Tempo's population of 284 consisted of 166 females and only 118 males; and while the proportions may have been somewhat different outside the village, where there was more employment for farm labourers, many of these photographs show women, children and old men.

Killyculla farmer's children, 1899.

Killyculla farmer and his family, 1899.

Mrs Ferry and her children,
Tempo, 1899.

Joseph Shannon and his children in the
turf bog, October 1899.

Francis Owens ('Pincher'), Killyculla, 1899.

Old man named Campbell, October
1899.

'M. Memier and children, September 1899'. The old woman's name is a puzzle. Not only are there no Memiers in the district nowadays, but there is not a single person of the name in the Irish telephone book, north or south.

Potato picker named McCaffrey, near Tempo,
1 November 1899.

Mrs Ferris, October 1899. The barefoot
girl on the left may have been a servant in
this relatively prosperous family.

Edward Doynien ('Coigher'), October 1899. The nickname may be a version of Cahir, the Irish for Charles or, less probably, a corruption of an Irish word meaning left-handed.

'Buying chickens', at Tempo Manor, October 1899. The cook is examining one of the old woman's birds, which were sold live. They were transported in the covered baskets, legs trussed.

'Tom Carland and his father digging spuds', October 1899.

Willie Doherty, June 1903.

'Stoving out rabbits, October 1897: Willie and Jimmy Ferris, Nelson and old Ferris'. Willie Ferris (left) has a pair of bellows under his arm to blow smoke down the rabbit burrows.

Two worlds meet: Mrs Cavendish Butler (Jenny Langham's mother) and Mrs Britten, 12 July 1900.

The reality of rural life: a cottage near Tempo, 4 August 1900. It has been estimated that forty years later 96 per cent of rural houses in County Fermanagh still had no running water; many had no convenient source of drinking water either. The crumbling gable wall of this cottage is propped up by flying buttresses of bog oak.

THE LANGHAMS ON THEIR TRAVELS

LIKE ANY family albums, those of the Langhams contain plenty of snapshots taken when they were away from home. Some of these show themselves and their friends in other parts of County Fermanagh, or at Portaferry in County Down where Cecily Langham lived. Many were taken much farther afield, however, for the Langhams travelled extensively in Europe—particularly in the south of France—for many years both before and after the great war, in search of butterflies for their collection. The quality of some of these Kodak snaps is particularly good, perhaps because the sunlight in Europe was rather more reliable than it was at home.

High cross and church at Drumcliff, County Sligo, 1910. In that year the Langhams visited Bundoran (a popular resort for well-to-do visitors from Fermanagh since the early years of the nineteenth century) and travelled by car to places of interest in the area.

Luncheon in the launch, at Knockninny on Upper Lough Erne, August 1900. Jenny Langham's mother remarried after the death of her first husband Sir William Emerson Tennent. Her second husband, Cavendish Butler, owned the island of Inishrath, where the Langhams were frequent visitors. Knockninny, nearby, had a landing stage for the steamers of the passenger service that ran up and down the lough at the turn of the century.

Portaferry, County Down, c 1910. The Langhams were related to the Nugent family and often visited Portaferry House. Charles Langham's sister Cecily lived for many years at Rockfield Cottage nearby.

Members of the Nugent
family and visitors in front
of Portaferry House in
1910. Both the boy on the
left and the girl on the right
are holding cameras.

Colbert the chauffeur and a splendid Léon Bollée car in front of Portaferry House, 1910. The registration is an early London one.

A 60 h.p. Mercedes belonging to Campbell Muir, photographed when passing through Newry on the way to Cork, 8 July 1903. Muir had just won a hill-climbing competition in this monster.

'The photographers
photographed': Jenny and
Cecily Langham with their
box cameras.

Winnie and Marion
Bowlby, daughters of
friends of the Langhams, at
Westgate-on-Sea in May
1910.

'Jenny at lunch on Colline St. Jean', 9 March 1901. This photograph was taken during a visit to Hyères, near Toulon in the south of France. There are butterfly nets lying on the ground. Jenny, an advanced young woman, is smoking a cigarette.

Loading wine at Hyères,
March 1901.

Dutch fishing boats on the
beach at Visscherspinken, 8
August 1901.

'Canal scene, The Hague, 8 August 1901.

Street scene in Ajaccio,
Corsica, April 1913.

Old woman in Ajaccio, April 1913. This is just the sort of picture the Langhams might have taken at home in Tempo.

ACKNOWLEDGEMENTS

This book could not have appeared without the interest and active assistance of a number of people. First and foremost thanks are due to the Langham family—to Sir James Langham for generously giving permission to copy and publish the photographs; to his mother Rosamond Lady Langham for her kindness in showing me things of interest in Tempo House; and to the younger Lady Langham in particular, for all her help with photographs and family papers. They have all been most kind and hospitable.

Thanks are also due to the Trustees of the Ulster Museum and to Bill Porter and his colleagues in the Museum's photographic department, since most of the photographs in this book were first brought to the notice of the public in an Ulster Museum travelling exhibition entitled 'Heydays, Fair Days and Not-so-good Old Days'.

For permission to use the Tennent papers, and to reproduce the picture of the Maguire house at Tempo and the map of the demesne, I have to thank Sir James Langham and the Director of the Public Record Office of Northern Ireland, where the Tennent papers are deposited.

Lastly, this book owes its appearance at such a reasonable price to the generous support of Fermanagh District Council. The Council is to be congratulated on helping to make these glimpses of old Fermanagh more widely known. I am also happy to record my gratitude to the Clerk to the Council, Mr Gerry Burns, for his interest and for his help in arranging this sponsorship.

Ulster Museum, Belfast
August 1986

SOURCES

The main manuscript sources for the history of the Maguires are pedigrees of the family in the Genealogical Office, Dublin and the entries in the Registry of Deeds, Dublin; for the Tennents and Langhams, the Tennent papers in the Public Record Office of Northern Ireland, Belfast.

So far as printed sources are concerned, see particularly P. O Gallachair's article 'The first Maguire of Tempo' in *Clogher Record* vol. II, no. 3 (1959); Joan Trimble's article 'Carolan and his patrons in Fermanagh and neighbouring areas' in *Clogher Record* vol. X, no. 1 (1979); Lady Cathcart's obituary in the *Gentlemen's Magazine*, vol. lix, pt. 2 (August 1789) and the references to her in Maria Edgeworth's *Castle Rackrent*, ch. ii; Brian Maguire's *Memoirs*; O'Donovan's ordnance survey letters on Fermanagh 1834-5; and the entry for Sir James Emerson Tennent in the *Dictionary of National Biography*.